ISAAC ASIMOV'S
Library of the Universe

Projects in Astronomy

by Isaac Asimov

Gareth Stevens Publishing
Milwaukee

Library of Congress Cataloging-in-Publication Data

Asimov, Isaac, 1920-
    Projects in astronomy / by Isaac Asimov.
        p.   cm. — (Isaac Asimov's library of the universe)
    Includes bibliographical references.
    Summary: Presents a variety of astronomy projects, including creative writing and drawing assignments, modelmaking, sky observation, and experiments.
    ISBN 1-55532-401-0
    1. Astronomy projects—Juvenile literature. 2. Astronomy—Study and teaching (Elementary) [1. Astronomy projects. 2. Astronomy. 3. Science projects.] I. Title. II. Series: Asimov, Isaac, 1920- Library of the Universe.
    QB64.A75   1990
    372.3'5—dc20   89-43133

A Gareth Stevens Children's Books edition
Edited, designed, and produced by
Gareth Stevens, Inc.
RiverCenter Building, Suite 201
1555 North RiverCenter Drive
Milwaukee, Wisconsin 53212, USA

For a free color catalog describing Gareth Stevens' list of high-quality children's books, call 1-800-341-3569 (USA) or 1-800-461-9120 (Canada).

Cover art © Dan Burr

Astronomy projects editor: John D. Rateliff
Project editor: Mark Sachner
Series design: Laurie Shock
Book design: Kate Kriege
Picture editor: Matthew Groshek
Technical advisers and consulting editors: Julian Baum, Matthew Groshek, and Francis Reddy

Printed in the United States of America

1 2 3 4 5 6 7 8 9 96 95 94 93 92 91 90

CONTENTS

Nowadays, we have seen the known planets up close, all except for the farthest known planet, Pluto. We have mapped Venus through its clouds. We have seen dead volcanoes on Mars and live ones on Io, one of Jupiter's satellites. We have detected strange objects no one knew anything about till recently: quasars, pulsars, black holes. We have studied stars not only by the light they give out, but by other kinds of radiation: infrared, ultraviolet, x-rays, radio waves. We have even detected tiny particles called neutrinos that are given off by the stars.

Every day, astronomers and other scientists work to further understand the Universe. Reading about their strange discoveries is surely exciting, but doing your own science projects is the best way to understand how scientists think and work. Through the projects in this book, you will study the colors in sunlight, make craters, build a simple telescope, and more. It's your turn to be the scientist!

Isaac Asimov

Project 1:
A Letter Home

Long before the first rocket ever blasted off, artists and writers had already taken us into space. Artists combine scientific knowledge with imagination to show us landscapes no human eyes have yet seen.

Like artists, science fiction writers also create worlds that are part imagination and part science. It's fun to read old stories about space travel to see how right or wrong the author was.

Drawing and writing about space are both projects you can enjoy. Can you picture a sunrise on Mercury? How would you feel if you were the first astronaut to step onto the surface of Mars?

An artist imagines his own "island world" — a space station linked up to an asteroid to create a cosmic mining station.

Purpose of the project:
To write about and illustrate an imaginary trip to an alien world.

What you'll need:
•Pen and paper
•A typewriter (optional)
•Art supplies
•Your imagination

What to do:
We are living in the Space Age. Humans have walked on the Moon. We've sent probes beyond the Solar system. In your lifetime, people from Earth may reach other planets and even begin the first space colonies.

Imagine what it would be like to stand on the surface of another world. What would you see? If the other world is in our Solar system, what would the Sun and Earth look like from out there? If you have traveled beyond our Solar system, imagine the kinds of stars and planets you encounter. What kinds of life forms, if any, will you meet?

Pretend that you're writing a letter home. Describe what you see and feel. In your letter, you might want to include illustrations of what you find.

Instead of writing a letter, you may want to create out of your imagined experiences a short story, complete with illustrations.

Be as creative as you want. You can compare your imagined alien world with those of your friends. Or you might want to read several science fiction stories by different authors and illustrators and watch episodes of different science fiction television series or movies. How do these imagined worlds differ from yours? What do they have in common?

Project 2:
Creating a Martian Landscape

The planet Mars is now drier than the driest desert on Earth. Water would simply boil away in its thin atmosphere. But, as scientists learned in the 1970s, Mars was not always as we see it now. Space probes revealed dried-up river channels on the Red Planet's surface.

The channels were probably carved by brief, muddy floods, not true rivers as we have on Earth. Ice beneath the soil probably melted, creating a flow of mud and rock that etched the channels. By building a simple model of the Martian surface, you can study how it might be affected by flowing water.

This photograph, taken by a probe, shows a series of dried-up channels on Mars. The channels were probably caused by drainage long ago.

Purpose of the project:
To re-create the effects of erosion in order to understand how Mars' surface came to look the way it does today.

What you'll need:
• A waterproof box. This can be anything from a baking pan to a cut-down cardboard box lined with a plastic garbage bag. The experiment works best with a wide, shallow box.
• Water, and something to pour it from — either a garden hose or a large pitcher
• Several bricks or wooden blocks
• Sand and various sand-like materials, such as dirt, flour, or small rocks

What to do:
Fill the box with sand or dirt. Be sure to pack it in firmly. Set the box up at an angle, as shown in the picture, using the bricks or wooden blocks to hold it in position. The ground in front of the box is going to get wet, so be warned!

Turn on the hose or fill the pitcher. Start pouring water on the sand at the top of the box, gradually at first, then more. Watch how it cuts channels in the sand as it flows across the box.

When you have made a number of "valleys," turn off the water. Compare your landscape with the photograph of Mars. Do they look similar?

What happens if you freeze the box? Can you simulate a "Marsquake" by flexing it to crack the soil? Repeat the experiment with the water. How do the rifts you've caused affect the "rivers"?

Clean out the box and try the experiment again. This time add small rocks to the sand and watch how they divert the flow of the water. You might also like to try packing the sand loosely and watching how this speeds up the erosion. Finally, pack the box with alternating layers of sand, gravel, and other "soils." The resulting "Martian canyons" should show the different layers as strata, just like natural canyons here on Earth!

Project 3:
Do-It-Yourself Craters

The planets were formed as chunks of debris clumped together to form larger and larger chunks. Some of that debris still floats through the Solar system. When debris strikes a moon or planet, the impact gouges out a huge hole, or crater, in the surface.

There are only about 100 known impact craters still on Earth. Wind and rain have worn away all but the largest. But there are thousands on Mercury, Mars, Earth's Moon, and the many other moons in the Solar system. Impact craters are the main features on many of these worlds. In this project, you'll study how craters form.

When viewed from Earth, impact craters give the Moon its special appearance. This close-up shows the variety of sizes and styles of lunar craters.

Purpose of the project:
To show how meteorite craters are formed and understand the different shapes they take.

What you'll need:
•A waterproof box, just like the one used in Project 2: "Creating a Martian Landscape"
•Dirt and flour
•Water and a watering can
•Several pebbles or marbles
•A chair or stepladder

What to do:
Place your box flat on the ground and fill it up with dirt. Sprinkle water over the dirt until it has a nice mud-like consistency. Place a chair or stepladder next to the box and climb up on it.

Drop a few pebbles or marbles one by one into the mud. What kinds of craters do they make? Try throwing some so they hit at different angles. Throw some pebbles harder, some softer. Compare the result with the picture of the Moon on this page. Are the lunar craters different from yours?

To create a different effect, clean out the box, retrieve your "meteorites," and set up the experiment again. This time, try adding more water to make the mud much softer. Throw more "meteorites" in (look out for splashes!). Notice how the wetter mud beneath fills up all but the largest craters, just like the "seas" on the Moon.

Set up the experiment again, without any water this time. Fill the box with layers of differently colored "soils" (for example, flour and dirt). Notice how the craters reveal the layer underneath and how some of the "soil" splashes out on the surface, just like the rays of the crater shown on this page.

Project 4:
Observing and Understanding the Earth-Moon System

Earth and Moon have been in a cosmic dance that has gone on for billions of years. The Moon appears to change its shape as it moves in its monthly orbit around Earth. It sometimes appears as a slim crescent and at other times as a bright white disk. These changes, called the Moon's phases, occur because every day we see a slightly different fraction of the Moon's sunlit side as it orbits Earth.

Studying an Earth-Moon model makes the Moon's phases much easier to understand. But don't forget to observe the real thing! A newspaper can tell you when to look.

Purpose of the project:
To observe the phases of the Moon and understand what causes them.

What you'll need:
•Paper and pencil
•A small white ball, like a Ping-Pong ball
•A bright light, such as a street lamp or bulb without a shade
•Chalk or string
•A friend

What to do:
The Moon's appearance changes every night. By making a simple model you can see why the phases of the Moon are the result of the relationship between Earth, the Moon, and the Sun.

Look in a newspaper, calendar, or almanac to find out the date of the next new Moon. Several days after this date, look for the Moon near where the Sun has set. Note what part of the sky it's in and draw its shape. Also make notes of when it rises and sets. Repeat this the following night and every night for a month and continue to draw pictures of its changing phases. What discoveries did you make that surprised you?

To show how the Moon's phases work, create a model of the Sun, Moon, and Earth. First, make a circle near a strong light source. Stand or sit in the middle of the circle. The lamp represents the Sun, you represent Earth, and the circle represents the Moon's path around Earth. Have a friend hold the Ping-Pong ball — the "Moon" — so the light shines on it. While your friend walks around the circle, watch the changing shape of the lighted portion of the ball. Compare it with the sketches of the Moon you made earlier.

Repeat the experiment, this time letting your friend sit while you play "Moon." See if you can cause any solar and lunar "eclipses." Important: This experiment will work only if you have a single light source in an otherwise darkened room or area.

1   2   3   4

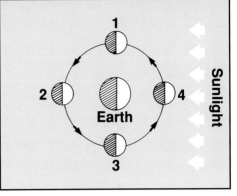

1

2   Earth   4

3

Sunlight

Above: The shape of Earth's Moon appears to change as it orbits our planet. These changes, called phases, occur because each day we see a slightly different fraction of the Moon's sunlit side. Right: A diagram representing the Earth-Moon system as viewed from above shows that the side of the Moon facing the Sun is always illuminated.

Key to the Moon's phases as viewed from Earth:

(1) first quarter   (3) last quarter
(2) full Moon   (4) new Moon

Project 5:
Solar System Sizes to Scale

The Solar system is our home. It consists of the Sun, nine known planets (including Earth), dozens of moons, thousands of asteroids, and perhaps billions of distant comets. The part we know most about extends from the Sun out to Pluto. The innermost planets — Mercury, Venus, Earth, and Mars — are made mostly of iron and rock. The next four — giant Jupiter, Saturn, Uranus, and Neptune — are huge balls of gas. Far-flung Pluto is an oddity, a tiny frozen gas ball.

You'll need plenty of space for this project, which will help you appreciate just how big our Solar system really is.

Purpose of the project:
To understand the incredible size of the Solar system by making a model to scale.

What you'll need:
- A large beach ball
- A pea
- A tape measure
- A friend
- A large open area, like a baseball field or empty parking lot

What to do:
Most models of the Solar system make the planets seem far bigger and closer together than they really are. But compared to the vastness of space, the planets are incredibly small and far apart.

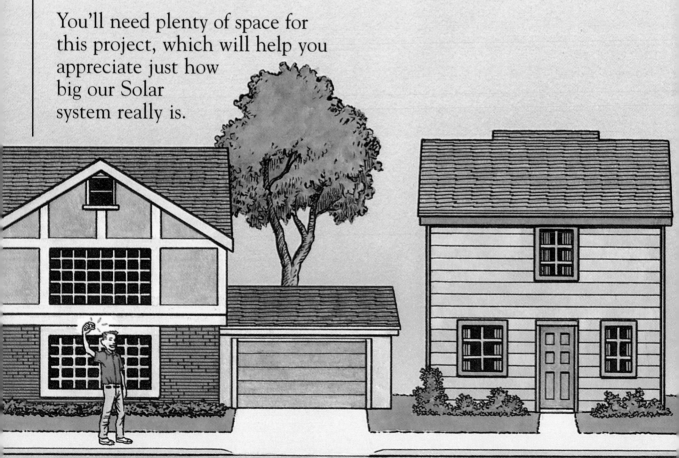

To show this, give your friend the beach ball and have him or her stand at one end of the field. Put the pea in your hand, and using the tape measure, pace off 200 feet (61 m). Turn around and look back. If the Sun were the size of your friend's beach ball, Earth would be the size of the pea, and the distance between the two of you is how far apart the two would be.

To make a complete model of the Solar system would take a lot of friends and a very big field. For instance, "Mercury" would be a grain of sand in your hand about 80 feet (24 m) from the beach-ball Sun. That's nearly the distance from base to base on a baseball diamond. Grapefruit-size "Jupiter" would be over 1,000 feet (305 m) from the "Sun." That's almost as long as three football fields laid end to end. And "Pluto," the tiniest and most distant, would also be a grain of sand, a mile and a half (2.4 km) from the "Sun"!

If you can find a big enough area, you might want to get together with some friends and play the roles of Mercury, Earth, and Jupiter. Line up the correct distances away from the beach-ball Sun and start walking around it in your "orbits." Who finishes first? Check an encyclopedia and see how your results compare with the time it takes each of the real planets to make one orbit.

Project 6:
The Spectrum —
All the Colors of Light

Light from the Sun looks white to your eyes, but it is really a combination of many colors. These colors reveal themselves only when sunlight passes through a substance that causes it to bend. The different colors in sunlight do not bend by the same amount, and a rainbow pattern of color appears — red and orange, yellow to green, blue to violet. This display of colors is called a spectrum.

Light is only the visible portion of the larger electromagnetic spectrum, which includes x-rays and ultraviolet radiation, heat and radio waves. Keep this in mind as you make your own spectrum in this project.

A rainbow is a spectrum caused by sunlight passing through droplets of water in the air. This double rainbow was photographed over the Badlands, in South Dakota.

Purpose of the project:
To refract, or bend, light, showing how sunlight is actually made up of many different colors.

What you'll need:
• A shallow bowl
• Water
• A small mirror
• Sunlight
• A white wall or white poster board
• A garden hose attached to a faucet
• A small stone or lump of clay

What to do:
In this experiment we're going to create a spectrum out of sunlight. The diagram on the next page gives you an idea of how to arrange the different items in this project. First, fill up the bowl with clean water. Place the bowl in direct sunlight. Put a small mirror in the bowl, using the small stone or lump of clay to hold the mirror upright. Arrange the mirror so it reflects the light onto the wall. If you don't have a white wall to use, make a viewing screen by taping a piece of white poster board where the reflected light falls.

In combination with the mirror, the water should act as a prism to break up the white sunlight and project a many-colored spectrum. What colors do you see on your wall? What is their order?

If you have ever seen a rainbow, you have been treated to a naturally occurring spectrum. Rainbows are caused by sunlight passing through drops of rain in the air. The moisture acts like a prism and breaks up the sunlight into the colors of the spectrum. You can make your own miniature rainbow with a garden hose and a sunny day. Turn on the water and cover the end of the hose with your thumb to create a fine mist. Stand so that the Sun is directly behind you and point the water away from the Sun. With just a little maneuvering around, you should be able to spot a spectrum shimmering in the spray coming from the hose — your own private rainbow!

sunlight

mirror

water

stone

spectrum

Project 7:
Observing Meteor Showers

Some night when you're out under a clear, dark sky, you may be surprised to see one or more bright streaks. Most will disappear so fast that they'll be gone before you can tell anyone else where to look. But a few will last several seconds, lighting up the landscape and trailing smoke. These are meteors, flaming encounters between small, fast-moving space debris and Earth's atmosphere.

Several times a year Earth runs through the extra-dusty orbit of a comet. The dust creates a meteor shower, and your chances of seeing meteors increase greatly. You won't believe it until you see it!

A blazing meteor is caught by the camera as it flashes through the starry sky.

Purpose of the project:
To observe a meteor shower.

What you'll need:
- A dark sky and a comfortable place to lie down, such as a lawn chair
- An almanac to tell you when to look, and a star map to show you where
- Depending on the weather, a warm blanket or insect spray
- A friend to watch the night sky in the opposite direction

What to do:
Meteors streak through the atmosphere all the time — even during the day, when we can't see them. With any luck, you might see one some night when you're out stargazing. But sometimes many meteors appear on the same night. This is called a meteor shower. Here are some of the better known meteor showers, along with the constellations from which they seem to radiate:

Quadrantid (Boötes) January 1-4
Lyrid (Lyra) April 19-23
Perseid (Perseus) August 10-14
Orionid (Orion) October 18-23
Leonid (Leo) November 14-20
Geminid (Gemini) December 10-15
(Check the almanac to see when other showers occur.)

Pick a dark spot where it's safe and you won't be disturbed. Sit down, lean back, and let your eyes adjust to the dark. This is a good time to try to find some familiar constellations. Remember that any light, even moonlight, makes it much harder to spot meteors.

Don't expect the whole sky to light up — even the biggest showers usually only have one or two meteors a minute, and you can't watch the whole sky at once.

After this, all you do is relax and enjoy the show. You might want to invite some friends over and have a meteor-shower party — but don't get so involved visiting that you forget to keep looking up! Have a contest over who can spot the most.

Project 8:
Making Your Own Telescope

The first telescope was made in Holland in 1609. It was a simple combination of lenses that magnified distant objects so that they appeared to be nearby. An Italian scientist named Galileo Galilei heard about the invention and made his own. Galileo pointed his telescope at the Sun, Moon, and the planet Jupiter. He became the first astronomer to use a telescope.

That happened nearly 400 years ago. Since then, astronomers have developed telescopes that sense heat, ultraviolet radiation, and x-rays. Telescopes have even flown into space, where Earth's dirty atmosphere cannot spoil the view. You can make your own small telescope.

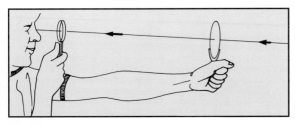

Before assembling your telescope, you can experiment with your two lenses to make the simple "open-air" telescope shown here. To focus, simply move the lenses forward and back.

Purpose of the project:
To build a simple telescope or spyglass.

What you'll need:
•Two magnifying glasses, one with a long focus and one with a short focus (explained below)
•Two cardboard tubes of different sizes that slide together snugly
•Tape (or glue), scissors, ruler, white cardboard

What to do:
Take the lens out of each magnifying glass. Find the focal length of each lens. This is the distance from the lens to the point where it clearly focuses an image. The best way to find the focal length of a lens is to take the lens outside and use it to project an image of the Sun onto a piece of sturdy white cardboard. When the Sun appears as a sharp point of light (see the illustration on the next page), the lens is the correct distance away. Use a tape measure or ruler to measure the focal length.

> **WARNING:**
> **NEVER look at the Sun, because doing this can make you blind. Also, beware of leaving its image focused on the paper for too long, as doing this could start a fire.**

Take the lens with the longer focal length and tape it or glue it firmly into the end of a tube. This lens is called the objective lens. Take the lens with the shorter focal length and tape or glue it firmly into the smaller tube. This lens is called the eyepiece. The length of each tube should be slightly shorter than the focal length of the objective lens. Fit the two tubes together with the lenses at opposite ends, as shown in the picture.

Now that you have your telescope, try it out. Look through it at some distant object. Slide the tubes back and forth until what you're looking at comes into focus. What details can you see through the telescope that you couldn't make out with your unaided eyes? Experiment with your telescope to see how far you can see.

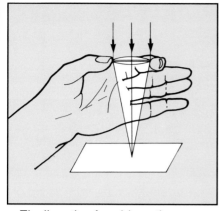

Finding the focal length.

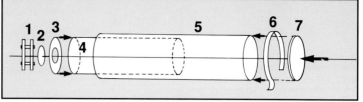

The key parts of your telescope: (1) tape (or glue); (2) short-focal-length lens (eyepiece); (3) if necessary, cardboard disk with hole cut out, for fitting lens into tube; (4) smaller tube, which should fit snugly into (5) larger tube; (6) tape (or glue); (7) long-focal-length (objective) lens.

Project 9:
Astronomy with Binoculars

It isn't necessary to get a fancy telescope to start investigating the night sky. One piece of equipment many people already own — binoculars — can show you some delightful astronomical sights. Binoculars show a larger piece of the sky than a telescope, and they can be carried along on any trip.

What can you see in the sky with binoculars? An up-close view of the Moon's cratered face or the four largest moons of Jupiter are easy targets. When viewed through binoculars, bright star clusters reveal dense fields of stars, and what look like fuzzy greenish stars turn out to be gas clouds called nebulas. Find some binoculars and try them out!

Two views of the Pleiades, one as seen with the unaided eye (lower left), the other as viewed through a pair of binoculars (lower right). This star cluster is also known as the Seven Sisters. The binoculars reveal more — and fainter — stars in the cluster, including a seventh "sister" that is too faint to be detected by the naked eye.

Purpose of the project:
To use binoculars to look at the night sky and observe the Universe.

What you'll need:
• A good pair of binoculars
• A clear night
• A dark place to observe from
• Also useful: an almanac and star wheel or star map to show you where to look

What to do:
When using binoculars, be sure to sit or stand in a comfortable position. If you can, rest your elbows or lean against a fence or tree to steady yourself.

Look at the Moon and compare what you see with your drawings from Project 4, "Observing and Understanding the Earth-Moon System." What new features can you make out? Use an almanac or newspaper to find out which planets are now visible, or if there are any upcoming eclipses of the Moon. Can you find Jupiter's moons or the phases of Venus?

Now let's go hunting for stars, galaxies, and nebulas. Locate the Pleiades (the Seven Sisters) or any other star cluster. Then compare what you see with and without your binoculars. Do the same with the three stars that make up Orion's sword. One of them is a star-birthing nebula — can you tell which? Look for other nebulas on your star map.

See if you can tell which star in the Big Dipper is really a double star — two for the price of one. Are there any other double stars? Look at the Milky Way. What features show up that aren't visible without the binoculars? Can you find any of its dark nebulas?

Finally, try to locate the Andromeda Galaxy, the farthest object we can see without a telescope. To the unaided eye, it's just a dim, misty spot in the darkness. But with binoculars and a bit of luck, you should be able to see it more clearly, from where we sit here on Earth, 2.3 million light-years away.

Project 10:
Building a
Constellation Projector

Nowadays city lights dim our view of the stars. For many people, a visit to a planetarium is the only way to see a bright, starry sky. A planetarium projects light through thousands of tiny holes onto a domed ceiling. Each hole represents a star in a constellation. The planetarium can re-create a starry sky as seen from any place on Earth –– and for any night during the next 26,000 years!

Planetariums help people identify and learn the constellations. You can construct a homemade planetarium from materials around the house. Once you've mastered the constellations, use your planetarium to teach your friends.

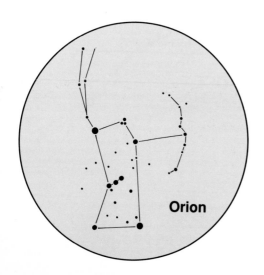

Orion

Purpose of the project:
To design and build a homemade planetarium.

What you'll need:
- A flashlight
- Dark cardboard
- Scissors
- Tape
- A pushpin
- A pencil
- A star map
- Black paper or paint
- An aluminum can (or cardboard tube)

What to do:
Unscrew and remove the flashlight lens (see item 1, next page). Paint the reflector black or cover it with black paper and reassemble the flashlight (see item 2).

Take a can. Remove the top and bottom. Tape over the sharp inside edges. Either paint the inside black or line it with black paper. Cut out a piece of dark cardboard and fit it into the can's bottom. Also cut a hole in it to fit around the flashlight. Tape over any cracks that would let light through.

Now you have your projector (see item 3) and are ready to make your constellation disks. Cut several disks out of the cardboard, each large enough to completely cover the open end of the can. Draw constellations on them from your star map, or photocopy the disks on these pages and use them as models. Using the pushpin and pencil, carefully make a hole where each star should be. For the brighter stars, make larger holes. Tape a disk into place, making sure no light gets out except through the star-holes. When you place the disk into the projector, be sure that the star patterns are not projected backwards!

Now you're ready to try it out. Take your projector into a darkened room and shine it on a wall. It will help you spot night-sky constellations by making you more familiar with them. You can also have fun with it. Put on an indoor show for your family and friends. You can also visit a planetarium and see how they project the night sky. Look at a star map and make up your own constellations to replace the traditional ones. Make disks for them and name them. See if you and your friends come up with the same patterns.

Project 11: Building a Sundial

Today we rely on clocks to tell us when to work, eat, and sleep. Early people figured out the time of day by observing the Sun's position in the sky and by using special devices called sundials that cast a shadow. As the Sun appeared to move across the sky, the shadow on the sundial moved along its clock face. In fact, a few hundred years ago, when people began to carry watches, you might have seen the now unusual sight of someone setting a watch to the time on a sundial!

Stonehenge, a stone monument near Salisbury, England, that is thousands of years old. Its precise alignment in relation to the rising and setting Sun has led many to wonder whether it might have been an ancient calendar.

Purpose of the project:
To learn to tell time from the Sun by building your own sundial.

What you'll need:
• A sunny outdoor spot
• A pencil or marker
• A foot-long (30-cm) dowel
• A compass
• A large sheet of white cardboard or paper
• A reliable watch or clock

What to do:
Find a level spot that's in direct sunlight for most or all of the day. Cover it with the cardboard or paper. Take your dowel and drive it through the cardboard into the ground. Make sure that it's standing up straight and the cardboard is flat.

Look on the cardboard to see where the shadow of the dowel falls. Every hour on the hour, mark the paper at the end point of the shadow. **NOTE: Be sure not to move the cardboard as you mark it.**

You now have a primitive clock. Repeat the experiment with the same piece of cardboard for several days to make sure all your markings are in the right place. You can use the compass to make sure that you line up the cardboard so it is facing the same direction every day. Then label each hourly marking (noon, one o'clock, two o'clock, and so forth).

Wait several months, then set up your sundial again. Have the shadows changed? What effect does daylight saving time or the changing of the seasons have on your sundial? Can you think of any places on our planet where a sundial wouldn't work? Why not? Do you think a moondial or stardial could be an accurate timekeeper?

Project 12:
Observing Sunspots the Safe Way

The Sun was once thought to be perfect in every way. In 1610, Italian scientist Galileo Galilei used his crude telescope to prove otherwise. He saw small dark spots on the Sun's surface. We know now that sunspots are cooler, stormy areas that don't shine as brightly as the rest of the Sun. Since the Sun is the nearest star, astronomers can detect details too small to see on any other star. But the Sun's brilliance can permanently damage our eyes and our instruments, so astronomers use special equipment to view it safely. This project helps you safely search for sunspots.

By projecting the Sun's image on a card, an astronomer plots the position of sunspots.

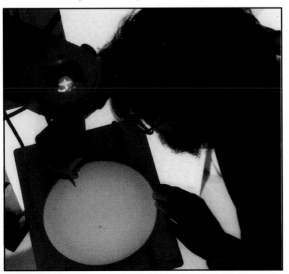

Purpose of the project:
To observe the Sun safely by using binocular projection.

WARNING: NEVER LOOK DIRECTLY AT THE SUN. NEVER LOOK AT THE SUN THROUGH A TELESCOPE OR BINOCULARS.

What you'll need:
- Masking tape
- Scissors
- A pair of binoculars
- White cardboard
- Something to hold the binoculars in place, like a tripod, a chair, or a wooden stand like the one shown at right

What to do:
If you've ever focused sunlight through a magnifying glass on a piece of paper, you know it's strong enough to set it on fire. Imagine focusing that kind of heat on your eye! **The only way to observe the Sun safely is indirectly, by projecting it through a set of lenses onto a screen, as in this project.**

Block off one half of the binoculars by taping a round white cardboard disk over the larger end, or objective lens (see item 1 on the next page). Then trace an outline of the smaller lens (eyepiece) onto some cardboard. Cut out the hole (2) and tape the cardboard securely onto or in front of the binoculars (3).

Find a sunny spot outdoors, or indoors near an open window. Fix the binoculars to a tripod, a chair, or a stand. Place another piece of white cardboard about a foot (30 cm) behind the binoculars (4). Adjust the focus of the binoculars until the Sun's image becomes clear (5). If you are indoors, a darkened room will help you see more detail.

Look carefully at the screen. Can you see sunspots or any other details? Place a piece of paper over the Sun's image on the screen and trace what you see. Repeat the experiment on several consecutive days and compare the drawings you've made. Do the sunspots move from day to day? What might this mean about the Sun's motion?

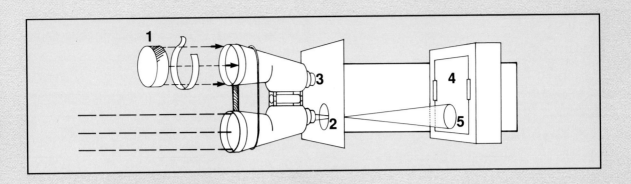

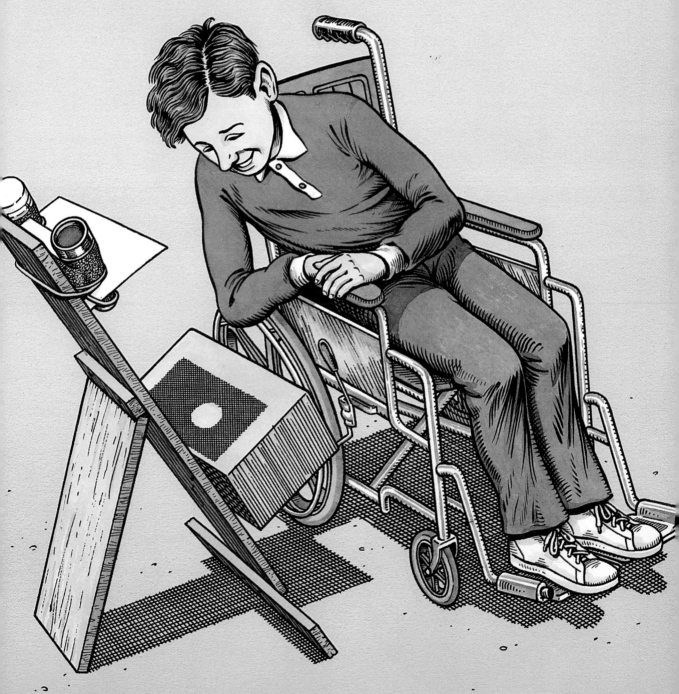

Project 13:
Time Capsules

We cannot travel any farther into the future than our own lives take us, and we cannot return to the past. But one clever idea accomplishes a little of both. It's called a time capsule — a sealed box into which people put all sorts of things that are important to them. They bury the box and wait for people to discover and study it in the future.

The greatest time capsules may be the Voyager 1 and 2 space probes. Each holds a recording of music and voices, and over 100 images of Earth. Future travelers may one day find it deep in space and learn more about us.

The jacket of the Voyager interstellar record, "The Sounds of Earth," gives instructions for playing the record and plotting Earth's present position in the Milky Way Galaxy.

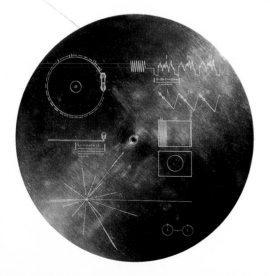

Purpose of the project:
To put together a packet of things to send into the future.

What you'll need:
- Almost anything, really — your choice of objects, papers, toys, cards, pictures, books, or other things that might tell someone something about you.
- A suitable container, preferably one that is airtight and watertight. A metal box is best, but anything from a jar to a shoe box will do if you keep it in an appropriate place.

What to do:
You don't need a time machine to go into the future; we're all traveling there together. One of the best ways to send a piece of the present into the future is with a time capsule. This is a box that is sealed and opened again at some specified time years later. Inside can be almost anything — a photograph of your best friend, a current newspaper, a recording of a hit song, a favorite toy, a letter, or whatever else you like.

To make your own time capsule, think about what you'd like someone in the future to know about what it was like to live in our times. Make a list of things you think they might be interested in. See how many of them you can gather. Seal them in a box and put it away in a safe place where no one will disturb it. Write on the outside when you want your time capsule to be opened.

A time capsule is like a message in a bottle from you to someone in the future — maybe even yourself when you're grown up. Try to think of what you'd like to find in a time capsule from your parents' or grandparents' time. You might want to discuss this project with your friends or your class at school and do it as a group project, having everybody put in one thing. Imagine what the people opening it will think of all they find! What could they find out about you from the things inside?

For More Astronomy Projects

Here are more books that contain scientific projects and lists of places to look for ideas and equipment. Check your local library or bookstore.

Astronomy Projects for Young Scientists. Apfel (Arco)
Far Out: How to Create Your Own Star World. West (Carolrhoda Books)
Look to the Night Sky: An Introduction to Star Watching. Simon (Penguin)
Magic Mud and Other Great Experiments. Penrose (Simon & Schuster)
Projects in Space Science. Gardner (Julian Messner)
Science Fare: An Illustrated Guide and Catalog of Toys, Books, and Activities for Kids.
        Saul and Newman (Harper & Row)
The Space Spotter's Guide. Asimov (Gareth Stevens)
3-D Star Maps. Monkhouse and Cox (Harper & Row)
Whitney's Star Finder. Whitney (Knopf)

In addition to these and other books, many science magazines feature projects. Here are a few to look for in your library: *National Geographic World, Odyssey, Owl, Ranger Rick, Science World,* and *3-2-1 Contact.*

For Catalogs from Science Supply Companies

The following companies can send you catalogs full of information, equipment, and ideas for science projects. When you write to them, be sure to tell them exactly what you want to know about. And always include your full name and address.

Delta Education
P.O. Box M
Nashua, New Hampshire 03061

Sargent-Welch Scientific Company
7300 North Linden Avenue
Skokie, Illinois 60076

Nasco Science
901 Janesville Road
Fort Atkinson, Wisconsin 53538

Edmund Scientific Company
Attention: Marketing Dept., MB
101 East Gloucester Pike
Barrington, New Jersey 08007

For Up-to-Date Sky-watching Information

Astronomical "Hotline"
(Toronto, Ontario)
Dial (416) 586-5751

"Skyline"
(Cambridge, Massachusetts)
Dial (617) 497-4168

"Sky Report"
(Los Angeles, California)
Dial (213) 663-8171

Long-distance charges apply to all of these numbers. For a fuller listing of astronomical update phone lines, consult the September 1989 issue of *Sky and Telescope* magazine in your library.

Glossary

alien: in this book, a being from some place other than Earth.

atmosphere: the gases that surround a planet, star, or moon.

channel: a groove, usually formed by running water, that runs in or through something.

constellation: a grouping of stars in the sky that seems to trace out a familiar figure or symbol. Constellations are named after the shapes that people think they resemble.

crater: a hole or pit on a planet or moon created by volcanic explosions or the impact of meteorites.

dark nebulas: vast clouds of dust and gas that do not give off much light of their own or are too far from neighboring stars to reflect much light. Dark nebulas obscure portions of the Milky Way from our view.

diameter: the length of a straight line through the exact center of a circle or sphere.

eclipse: the partial or complete blocking of light from one astronomical body by another.

erosion: the process of being worn away bit by bit, usually by wind or water.

focal length: the distance from the surface of a lens to the point of its focus, or focal point.

light-year: the distance that light travels in one year — nearly six trillion miles (9.6 trillion km).

meteor: a meteoroid that has entered Earth's atmosphere in a fiery blaze. Also, the streak of light made as the meteoroid enters or moves through the atmosphere.

meteorite: a meteoroid when it hits Earth.

meteoroid: a lump of rock or metal drifting through space. Meteoroids can be as big as asteroids or as small as specks of dust.

nebula: a cloud of dust and gas in space. Some large nebulas, or nebulae, are the birthplace of stars. Other nebulae are the debris of dying stars.

orbit: the path that one celestial object follows as it circles, or revolves, around another.

phases: the periods when an object, such as Venus, Mercury, or our Moon, is partly lit by the Sun. It takes about one month for Earth's Moon to progress from full Moon to full Moon.

prism: a transparent object that breaks up white light into the colors of the spectrum.

refract: to bend or break up light as it passes through a prism.

"seas": the name for the flat dark areas on the Moon, even though they are completely waterless. Any one of these "seas" is actually called a "mare" (pronounced MAH-ray).

spectrum: the bands of color that appear when white light is broken up by a prism. You can see the colors of the spectrum in a rainbow.

sundial: an instrument to measure the time of day by the movement and location of the Sun.

Index

The publishers wish to thank the following for permission to reproduce copyright material: front cover, pp. 5, 7, 9, 11 (large), 12-13, 15 (large), 17, 19 (large), 21, 23 (large), 25, 27 (large), 29, © Dan Burr, 1990; p. 4, © Alan Gutierrez, 1986; pp. 6, 28, Jet Propulsion Laboratory; p. 8, © George East; pp. 11 (insets), 15 (inset), 18, 19 (insets), 20 (both), 22, 23 (insets), 27 (inset), Matthew Groshek, © Gareth Stevens, Inc., 1990; p. 14, © James R. Peterson, 1986; p. 16, © Dennis Milon, 1980; p. 26, courtesy of the National Solar Observatory, National Optical Astronomy Observatories.